JOHN NAPIER

JOHN NAPIER

LOGARITHM JOHN

LYNNE GLADSTONE-MILLAR

NATIONAL MUSEUMS OF SCOTLAND PUBLISHING

Published by NMS Publishing
a division of NMS Enterprises Limited
National Museums of Scotland
Chambers Street
Edinburgh EH1 1JF

ISBN 1-901663-70-1

British Library Cataloguing in Publication Data
A catalogue record of this book
is available from the British Library.

Cover design by Mark Blackadder.
Book design by Cara Shanley, NMS Publishing,
NMS Enterprises Limited.
Printed and bound in Great Britain by Bath Press Ltd, Bath.

Cover images: (Main picture) *John Napier*, artist unknown, reproduced by
permission of the University of Edinburgh; (inset) Napier's Bones,
courtesy of the Trustees of the National Museums of Scotland.

Frontispiece image: John Napier, from *An Account of the Life, Writings
and Inventions of John Napier of Merchiston*, 1787, NMS Library.

Motif used throughout: Seal of John Napier of Merchiston, from
Strathendrick and Inhabitants from Early Times, 1896.

CONTENTS

ACKNOWLEDGEMENTS

THE principal difficulty I had when writing this book was the necessity of mastering, once again, the mystery of logarithms. I should therefore like to express my particular appreciation to Marion Muetzelfeldt, Head of Mathematics at Merchiston Castle School, for so patiently re-introducing me to logarithms, and to John Buchanan who also came to the rescue. In addition, many others have also given generously of their time, and I would like to thank them here:

Andrew Digby of the Royal Observatory, Edinburgh
Dr Hugh Dinwoodie of the Edinburgh Archaeological Field Society
Dr Ronald W Hilditch, Director of Observatory, University of
 St Andrews
Pat and Charlie Napier
Members of the staff of Napier University, Edinburgh

I am also very grateful to the University of Edinburgh for permission to reproduce their portrait of John Napier (artist unknown) on the cover of this book.

Lynne Gladstone-Millar
January 2003

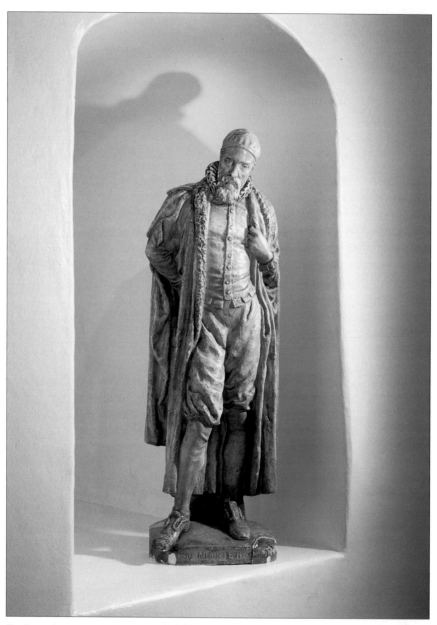

The nineteenth-century maquette made by David Watson Stevenson for the statue of John Napier that adorns the Scottish National Portrait Gallery in Edinburgh. (Photo: Niall Hendry; courtesy of Napier University, Edinburgh)

AN ASTONISHING WORLD

W HEN John Napier was born in 1550 in the medieval tower house of
Merchiston Castle near Edinburgh, he opened his eyes on to an astonishing world. Europe, having been set ablaze by the artists, architects, sculptors,
inventors and writers of the Renaissance, had also pushed out to new frontiers
in different fields. Copernicus had just proved that the sun was the centre of
the universe. Columbus had crossed the Atlantic. Vasco da Gama had sailed
round the Cape of Good Hope, finding a sea route to India; and Magellan had
set off, planning to circumnavigate the globe, a feat achieved by his surviving
captain, Juan Sebastiano del Cano.

Scotland, although on the geographical outskirts of this European
burgeoning, was not left behind. She now had universities at St Andrews,
Glasgow and Aberdeen, and her people were cosmopolitan. As early as the
1040s Macbeth, King of Scots, had mounted his horse and ridden to Rome,
and over the centuries the Scots had continued this great tradition of travelling, bringing back not only stories of what they had seen, but French and
Dutch tapestries, illuminated books, and sometimes even masons and

Merchiston Castle, Napier's home, where he finalised his calculations for logarithms.

1

The 'Lion Gate', Merchiston Castle. (NMS Library)

craftsmen to build their new homes and chapels. Only a few miles from young John's cradle at Merchiston Castle stood Roslin Chapel, which contains late Gothic carving in such elegance and profusion that it continues to bewilder the beholder today; and in the centre of Edinburgh the new graceful crown spire of the Kirk of St Giles, where the Napier family was buried, was a source of great pride to the townsfolk.

In the world of 1550, however, all the masons' measurements, all the merchants' accounts, and all the navigators' and astronomers' calculations, were laboriously worked out by long division and multiplication sums, squares and cubical extractions. It was a tedious, expensive and time-consuming process and, as Napier was later to point out, 'for the most part subject to many slippery errors'.

It was to be the destiny of John Napier to change all this. Watching his father, the Master of the Mint, dealing with the nation's finances, and at the other end of the scale seeing the shopkeepers in the luckenbooths at St Giles' struggling with their sums, John decided that somehow it should be possible to remove what he called 'those hindrances' – the long divisions and multiplications. With dogged tenacity he worked away all his adult life at the problem until it was almost an obsession. His first invention was logarithms, tables of numbers which, when read across, simplified multiplication and division, a version of which was used by every schoolchild as a shortcut in the mathematics classroom right up until the mid-1970s.

He also introduced the decimal point, which was less cumbersome than the decimal fractions that had been devised by the Flemish mathematician Simon Stevinus in 1585. Then came what was to be known universally as 'Napier's Bones', the *Rabdologia*, which was a method of calculation using small rods in a box.

Napier's logarithms were to the Elizabethan and Jacobean world what the computer is to ours. The Bones were to the masons, the merchants and the farmers what the pocket calculator is to us. From the *Rabdologia* quickly developed the slide-rule, a version of which was still being used by NASA engineers in the 1960s for the development of space travel.

Napier's invention was a quantum leap in mathematics comparable to the discovery by Archimedes in the second century BC of formulae for the areas and volumes of spheres and cylinders, and comparable with the introduction

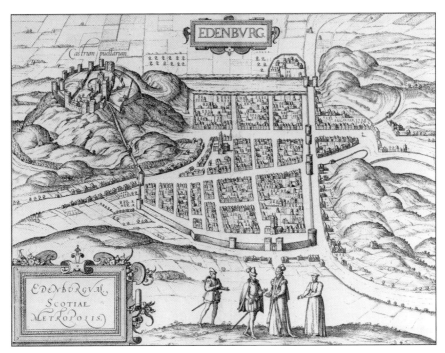

Napier's Edinburgh. Braun and Hogenberg print, late sixteenth century. (Courtesy of the National Gallery of Scotland)

of Hindu-Arabic numerals to Europe by Leonardo Fibonacci in AD 1202. And the extraordinary thing about Napier was, first, that he thought that his most important contribution to mankind was not in the field of mathematics at all, but a publication on religious philosophy and second, that his great mathematical discovery was made in comparative isolation in a tower house in Scotland. Although Scottish travellers brought home many of the glories of the Renaissance from Europe, they did not give a high priority to news of any mathematical research which was going on. Without the stimulation of this, Napier plodded on with his ideas and his figures, quite alone.

When John Napier's ancestor, Sir Alexander Napier, donated generously to the embellishment of St Giles' Cathedral in 1460, he had his own face sculpted on to a pillar at the east end. (Photo: John Arnott)

3

A PRIVILEGED BEGINNING

JOHN Napier's family was wealthy and privileged. His forebears could be traced back to 1068 when Archill of Northumbria, a supporter of the Anglo-Saxon claimant to the English throne, was on the losing side in a battle against William the Conqueror, and had to retreat north hurriedly to the safety of the court of the Scots king, Malcolm Canmore. (Edgar Atheling, the surviving Anglo-Saxon heir, was the brother of Margaret, Malcolm's queen.) The king dealt kindly with Archill and gave him land in Dunbartonshire, Stirlingshire and an area around Loch Lomond known as the Levenax, subsequently shortened to Lennox.

Documents from the time of King David I refer to Archill's grandson as the Earl of Lennox, and from then on the Lennox family were involved in all the machinations of the Scottish politics of the time. At the coronation of Robert the Bruce, a Lennox swore fealty to him, and a Lennox seal is on the Scottish Declaration of Independence drawn up at Arbroath in 1320. John Napier's connection to the Lennoxes was through Donald of Lennox, the seventh son of the second earl. It is at this point in the family tree that the name Napier first appears, but its spelling had not been settled upon by the family even 300 years later. They used Nepair, Naipper, Neper, Napper and Napare, and John was registered at St Salvator's College, St Andrews as Johannes Neaper. History seems to have settled for Napier.

By the beginning of the fifteenth century the Napiers were people of influence in Edinburgh, now the capital of Scotland. One had been governor of Edinburgh Castle, another a provost, and a third sent abroad by the king on embassies. Sir Alexander Napier, a benefactor of the Kirk of St Giles, even had the Napier shield of arms emblazoned on one of the pillars, and his own face sculpted by its side (see page 3).

The family were known for loyal service to the Crown. John's great grand-father had fallen fighting for his king at the Battle of Flodden in 1513, and his grandfather at the Battle of Pinkie in 1547. By 1565 the Lennoxes and the Napiers were two distinct branches of the family tree, but John could point to the Lennox side and claim as a distant relative Lord Darnley, the new husband of Mary, Queen of Scots. If he had trodden the path customary for young men in his position, John might have been a page of honour to Mary, Queen of Scots and later a courtier, or he might have studied for the law or for the Church, or spent his life on the family estates, seeing to their affairs. As a very young man, however, John had different ideas.

The Napiers' connection with Merchiston began when they acquired the lands from King James I by settling a royal debt. Archibald, John's father, was only 15 years old when he married Janet, the daughter of Francis Bothwell, and John was born at Merchiston Tower the next year. The family home was an

Lord Darnley, artist unknown. (Courtesy of the Scottish National Portrait Gallery)

imposing L-shaped tower house, with a parapet-walk around the roof. It stood outside the town, high above the burgh muir, and its six-foot wide walls were built not only to withstand the elements, but cannon balls in time of siege. A high barmkin wall at the base of the tower contained steps by which the drawbridge on the second floor was reached. Here there was the great hall with a musicians' gallery – the Napiers entertained in style. There were other public rooms on this floor, and the kitchen. Above were the sleeping rooms, and on ground level were the storerooms and stables for when it was necessary

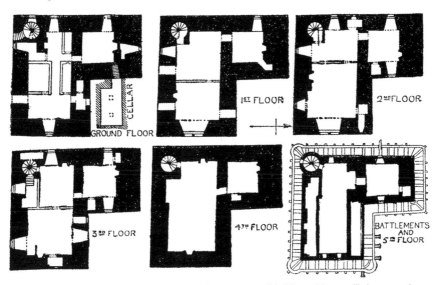

From its foundation in the fifteenth century Merchiston Castle was a grand building and it was still shown as such in the nineteenth-century drawings by MacGibbon and Ross in *Castellated and Domestic Architecture of Scotland.*

5

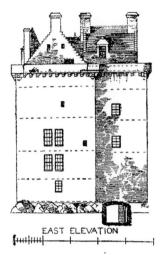

EAST ELEVATION

From MacGibbon and Ross.

to bring the cattle in. Spiral staircases within the walls connected each floor.

John's father became a Justice Depute, was knighted, and in 1582 was made Master of the Mint in Scotland, a post which also involved having responsibility for the mines and minerals in the land. John, being the eldest son, had a good education. In 1496 James IV, appreciating the importance of not only having priests who could understand the Latin of their offices, but also of having law-givers who could properly interpret the law, had an Act passed which required the gentry to send their eldest sons to a grammar school to learn Latin, and then to university to study law. Later, in 1560, the Reformation brought the First Book of Discipline with even more emphasis on education, 'Seeing that God hath determined that his Church here in earth shall be taught not by angels but by men ...'. There was to be a schoolmaster in every parish able to teach grammar and Latin, 'if the town be of any reputation'.

It was to be some time before this noble dream came to reality, but for John, with the High School of Edinburgh already well established, education was within reach. If he did not, in fact, attend the town's grammar school, he certainly had excellent tutors, for he was able to go to the University of St Andrews at the age of 13. This was not unusual in those days. The Faculty of Arts at St Andrews insisted that a 'determinant' – a student completing a first degree – had to be at least 15 years old, which meant that many students would have been 13 when they began their courses. Nevertheless, for John this big step must have been daunting. That year, 1563, was an anxious time. Scotland was in turmoil with the Reformation, and there were well-founded fears that the outbreak of plague in Europe, which had crossed the Channel and killed 20,000 in London, would soon creep north to Scotland. John had only been at St Andrews for three months when he received the news that his mother had died. Among her recorded debts was 'to Johnne Rutherfurde for hir sonnis burde, auchteen pundis' ('... for her son's board, eighteen pounds'). Not a good time for a 13 year-old to be away from his family and home.

Coming from a well-off family, however, John would ride up to St Andrews accompanied by a servant, their belongings strapped to a pack-horse. At least he would have a familiar face with him when he reported to his lodgings at the house of St Salvator's College Principal, John Rutherford, a man renowned for his good teaching and bad temper.

A VERY YOUNG STUDENT

CHILDREN grew up very quickly in the sixteenth century. In 1563 Charles IX of France was declared 'of age' at the age of 13, and that same year, at the same age, John Napier was considered old enough to go to St Andrews University. He would not be given much quarter for home-sickness or grief once there. He was looked after by servants who were men, except for the *lotrix*, the washerwoman, who had to be over 50 years of age.

The universities were in the forefront of all the controversies of the Reformation and when John entered the gates of St Salvator's College in North Street in 1563, he passed over the spot where Patrick Hamilton had been burnt at the stake as a heretic by the Roman Catholics in 1528. An equally gruesome place nearby was outside the castle, where George Wishart had suffered a similar fate only four years before John's birth.

Ambitious plans had been drawn up by the Reformers for the universities, but by 1563 they had, for the most part, not yet been carried out. Therefore the day-to-day routine of St Salvator's was much the same as it had always been. The college was run by the third- and fourth-year students, who took turns to be cup-bearer, under cup-bearer, butler, reader and under-reader. The students were read to at mealtimes, where the diet was rather repetitive – bread, broth, meat and fish. Vegetables from the college garden relieved the tedium. Being a religious foundation, the college still placed a high priority on the study of theology, and once a week a Master took charge of a theological debate which apparently could become rather heated. The debaters were encouraged 'not to bite and devour one another like dogs; but to behave as men desirous of mutual instruction, and as the servants of Christ, who ought not to strive, but to be gentle to all'.

The emphasis on the study of theology suited John, and the lack of a Chair of Mathematics appeared to be of no apparent loss to him. At this time, young though he was, he was drawn to the study of the biblical Apocalypse. In 1593, when he published his *Plaine Discovery of the whole Revelation of Saint John*, he was to refer in his preface to his 'tender yeares and bairneage in Sanct Androis' as the time when he was inspired to study the Apocalypse.

John also described the difficult circumstances he found himself in at that time. He 'on the one part contracted a loving familiaritie with a certaine gentleman, a Papist; and, on the other part, [was] attentive to the sermons of that worthy man of God, Maister Christopher Goodman, teaching upon the Apocalyps'. There had been 'continual reasoning' between Protestant John and his Roman Catholic friend, and the result was a firm resolution on John's part to study the 'remanent mysteries of that Holy Book'. This led to the publication of his *Plaine Discovery of the whole Revelation of Saint John*, a work which to the end of his days he held in higher regard than any of his mathematical discoveries.

The College of St Salvator, St Andrews, as it would have been in Napier's time. (Drawing: R G Cant; courtesy of St Andrews University Library on behalf of the Strathmartine Trust)

As with all the first-year students, John began his time at St Andrews as a 'bajan' – a *bec-jaune* or fledgling. (The present use of 'bejant' only began around 1800.) As such he would have had to endure an initiation devised by the senior students, which was almost as necessary as his matriculation.

The medieval college buildings had not changed much since their foundation by Bishop Kennedy in 1450, and John found himself in a cloister which had been damaged by a fire caused by the siege of the castle by French Roman Catholic troops in 1547, when John Knox was captured and chained as a slave in the French galleys. The timber spire on the tower of St Salvator's had been flattened in this battle, and was subsequently used by the troops as a gun platform for besieging the castle. By the time John reached the college, however, a spire had once again risen above the cloisters, this time in stone.

Most of the students lived in the cloisters, but there was also accommodation in a house attached to the west side of the tower and in a wing in Butts Wynd. Behind the tower was the Common School, and above this the Great Hall. It was not a large complex, and bajans soon found their way around it.

For the young bajans the curriculum was daunting. They were immediately plunged into the study of rhetoric and logic, and after this metaphysics, physics and the ethics of Aristotle. And, of course, they had to become fluent in Latin.

When John arrived at the university, fashion dictated that he would be wearing knee breeches, hose, a doublet (possibly with trunk sleeves) and a falling collar. Coming from a wealthy family as he did, his doublet might well have been padded and colourfully braided, and his bonnet trimmed with a drooping feather. Now, as a bajan, he was required to wear a girdled gown, and not to be too flamboyant with his clothes.

The college had its own collegiate church, a fine medieval building which still stands to this day. By the time John attended St Salvator's the Protestant Reformation had brought about many changes in the Catholic church buildings, and part of the college chapel became the St Andrew's Commissary Court. Occasional services were held in the church, and if John attended he would have seen the medieval consecration crosses still clearly visible on the walls, and the elaborate tomb of the founder, Bishop Kennedy.

St Andrews was a small town, and the students were well aware of the arrival of people of consequence. A staunch Reformer, even at the age of 13, John would have found the occasional visits of John Knox very exciting. The sovereign, Mary, Queen of Scots, stayed quite frequently. She came, probably to escape the rantings of John Knox in Edinburgh, and enjoyed her times in St Andrews, living comparatively informally in a merchant's house in South Street and filling her days with riding, hawking, archery, music and other courtly entertainments.

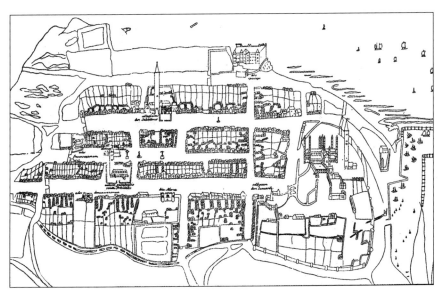

St Andrews, c.1530.

The students had their leisure activities as well. James Melvill, who was a student at St Andrews only a few years after John was there, wrote in his diary of his enjoyment in making music with friends, practising archery and playing golf, and taking part in what he called 'hand and Racket catches' – fives and tennis? Unlike John, James Melvill stayed the course and worked his way through the various stages of the four-year curriculum to become a Bachelor in his third year and a Magistrand in his fourth.

For John there were other plans. As early as 1560, when John was only ten years old, his uncle Adam Bothwell, the Bishop of Orkney, writing in the turmoil of the Reformation, had advised John's father, 'I pray you, Schir, to send your sone Jhone to the schuyllis; oyer to France or Flandaris; for he can leyr na guid at hame, nor get na proffeit in this maist perullus worlde, that he may be savet in it, that he may do frendis efter honour and profeit as I doubt not bot he will'.

Perhaps the leisure pursuits enjoyed by the students at St Salvator's were too much of a distraction for the young man, or perhaps the situation in Scotland was indeed judged to be 'maist perullus' – in any event, John's father took the advice of his brother-in-law and sent his son abroad.

St Andrews Cathedral before it became a ruin, as envisaged by Alan Sorrell. (Courtesy of Historic Scotland)

TRAVEL WAS NOT FOR
THE FAINT HEARTED

TRAVELLING abroad in 1564 was a dangerous business. Ships plied regularly between the continent and Leith, where John would surely have started his journey. The hazards began there too. The small ships often foundered in storms or were blown off course for days on end, and passengers were at serious risk of being attacked by pirates at sea or, once ashore, by highwaymen on the continental roads.

There is an account of one Fynes Moryson, a Cambridge student who went to the continent to study law only 27 years after John had set sail. He had an uncomfortably close encounter with pirates from Dunkirk. Storms also delayed his ship and it took ten very miserable days to reach the Netherlands. He could not afford to relax even after he had disembarked; Spanish free-booters roamed the coastal roads, delighting particularly in robbing the English travellers of everything they possessed. Moryson, however, was determined to outwit them. He put his gold in his shoes and travelled in disguise.

Piracy or shipwreck — the hazards of sixteenth-century sea travel were very real. (© National Maritime Museum, London. Ref. BHC0748)

In his journal he recorded his experiences:

> *So I bought an old Brunswicke thrummed hat, and made mee a poore Dutch suite,*
> *rubbing it in the dust to make it seem old, so as my Taylor said, he took more paines*
> *to spoyl it, than to make it. I bought me linnen stockings, and discoloured my face*
> *and hands, and so without cloake, or sword, with my hands in my hose, tooke my*
> *place in a poore waggon.*

His demeanour being that of a penniless young man, when he reached an inn
for the night he dared not reveal that he had the money to pay for a bed,
a decent meal and a bottle of wine, and was often forced to sleep on a bench.
When his clothes were wet through, he could not change them for fear that
'my inward garments better than my upper, should betray my disguise to the
freebooters' spies'.

No comforts awaited those who did reveal their gold in order to get a good
night's sleep, however. The beds in the inns were so filthy and flea-ridden that
travellers took linen shifts which they put on over their night clothes as some
form of protection, and had their underclothes lined with taffeta which
discouraged the lice. Some even took their own bed linen in their trunks.

The smell of the stabling below came up through the draughty floor-
boards, and the stench of the ordure in the streets seeped in through the
ill-fitting windows. Rooms, even beds, often had to be shared with strangers

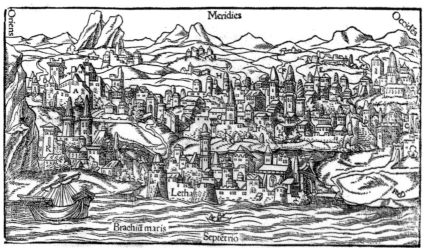

A	Palatium regis	B	Arx puellarum	C	Ecclefia S. Cutberti
D	Ecclefia S. Egidij	E	Minoritæ	F	Ecclefia beatæ Mariæ in cãpo
G	Collegium reginæ	H	Prædicatores	K	Monafterium S. Crucis

A last glimpse of Leith and Edinburgh from the River Forth — would young John ever see his home again?
(Sebastian Munster, late sixteenth century)

and, with fear of infection and misery with the bugs, some people preferred to sleep on a table or chest. Few reached the completion of their journeys unaffected by some misfortune.

Travel, therefore, was not for the faint hearted. Of course 14 year-old John would not have gone alone. He would have been accompanied by a servant, there to look after him and see to the chests containing his clothes, shoes, grammars, paper, ink, inkstand, pens and penknife. Possibly, at the beginning anyway, John would also have been accompanied by a tutor to help him negotiate the bribery pitfalls at the Customs and see to his study arrangements. It was expected that John would be away for a long time. When Adam Bothwell, the Bishop of Orkney, had advocated a period of study abroad for his nephew, he knew very well that this might mean a separation of several years for John and his family, and therefore much anxiety. The safe arrival of correspondence could never be guaranteed, and any news of a traveller's well-being, or otherwise was hard to come by. On the continent, as at home, people ran the daily risk of catching smallpox, typhoid, malaria and the plague. Life expectancy was short everywhere.

Documents tell us that John was back in Scotland at the age of 21, making the arrangements for his wedding, but nothing is on record of the years between his departure to the continent and that time. When he set off from his home at Merchiston Castle for Leith, however, his father Sir Archibald, his younger brother Francis and his sister Janet must have wondered when they would see him again – if ever.

It is not known where John went to study. The Bishop of Orkney had suggested that he should go to the schools of France or Flanders, but there is no proof that he did this. It is not recorded that he attended the University of Paris, nor indeed Bordeaux, Basel, Geneva, Amsterdam, Jena or Marburg. If he had gone to Paris, he would have found that Petrus Ramus, the Royal Professor of Philosophy and Eloquence, was not only deeply interested in mathematics and astronomy, but he was a Protestant – this was important to John. There was also in Paris a Professor of Mathematics, Carpentarius.

To venture to Rome would have been highly risky – the Inquisition there was vigorously persecuting Protestants, regarding them as heretics. It is tempting to think that John might have been attracted to Cracow, whose famous alumnus, Copernicus, had astonished the world some decades earlier by claiming, to his own great peril, that the Earth revolved daily on its axis, and annually round a stationary sun. However, in the matriculation books in the archives of the Jagiellonian University, Cracow, the name Napier of Merchiston does not appear, and it must be remembered that John had left St Andrews not with a burning ambition to study mathematics and astronomy, but to write on the Revelation of St John in the biblical Apocalypse.

To do this, Napier had to have an excellent knowledge of Hellenistic Greek, the Greek of the Bible. Mark Napier (as other writers have done) suggested in 1834 that Napier left St Andrews because it was difficult to study Greek there. There had been a time before the Reformation, he claimed, when the Roman Catholic Church frowned on the teaching of Greek:

> *The Bishop of Brechin, William Chisholm, hearing that* [George] *Wishart taught Greek New Testament in Montrose, summoned him to appear before him on a charge of heresy, upon which he fled the Kingdom. This was in 1538.* [It may, however, have been the contents of Wishart's lectures rather than the language he taught in that upset the Roman Catholic hierarchy.]

Nevertheless, if young John was anxious to study Hellenistic Greek, there is a compelling reason to think that he might have, at some time in his sojourn, gone to Geneva. In the 1560s many young Scots were drawn there to study, where they stayed with Henry Scrimgeour, a Scottish Professor of Arts who had himself been to St Andrews University. In addition, Christopher Goodman, who had influenced John so much at St Andrews, had fled from England to Geneva in 1553, fearing the Roman Catholic persecution of England's new queen, Mary Tudor. Finally, there was a well-known Greek scholar in Geneva at that time – Theodore Beza, Director of the Theological Academy which had been founded by John Calvin in 1559.

The fact that there are no records that Napier went to Geneva University, or indeed to any other one, however, does not mean that he did not go at all. He may have moved on from one university to another, and simply never matriculated at any of them.

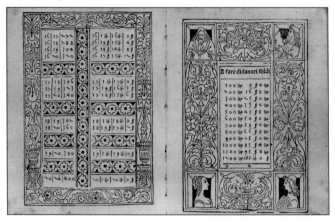

When travelling, John would see merchants using decorative books of mathematical tables and currency conversions to do their daily business. Woodcut in *Aritmetica* by Filippo Calandri, 1491. (Metropolitan Museum of Art, Rogers Fund, 1919. Ref. 19.24)

THE STUDENT COMES HOME

IN 1564, when Napier had gone to the continent as a boy of 14, he left a nation in turmoil. Only four years before, Protestantism had been officially established by the Scottish Parliament. However, the dissatisfaction with the status quo which led to the Reformation had been voiced for many years before – Patrick Hamilton, for instance, was burnt at the stake in 1528 for supporting 'divers heresies of Martin Luther and his followers'. The country was to remain in disarray for a long time after the Reformation. Napier arrived home to civil war.

There can be no generalisations as to why people joined the Reforming movement, for the Reformation was not only ecclesiastical. The whole structure of society in Europe was changing as merchants and craftsmen became wealthier and claimed a higher status in life. The hierarchical strangleholds of the feudal system, together with that of the Roman Catholic Church which had ruled them for centuries, were now challenged.

In Scotland there was an added dimension to the struggle – the presence of foreign troops. French soldiers were summoned by the Roman Catholic queen regent, Mary of Guise, the mother of Mary, Queen of Scots. As the Reformers' voices grew louder, she needed the French to prop up the authority of her government and the Roman Catholic Church. Therefore, in the Scottish Reformation it was not only religious fervour and a reaction against the feudal system that were factors, but also a genuine fear of repression by France. Earls, lairds, country-folk and town-dwellers had diverse reasons for throwing in their lot with the Reformers, and Napier's father was one of them. John too forsook his Roman Catholic upbringing and became a Protestant. In the ensuing struggle, supporters of the child-king James VI, who had been crowned in 1567 after abdication had been forced on his mother, were known as 'King's Men'. Those who sided with the imprisoned Mary, Queen of Scots were known as 'Queen's Men'.

Accusations flew about the land, and Sir Archibald Napier, although an avowed Reformer and King's Man, found himself being accused of disloyalty by both factions. As his brother-in-law had written some time before, he was 'sett amiddis betwix twa grete inconvenientis'. Certainly it must have been greatly inconvenient when he was restricted in 1568 from moving out of Edinburgh by the King's Men, and had to be prepared to appear before Regent Moray and the Lords of the Secret Council at six hours' notice.

The reason for this was that Merchiston Castle lay in a very strategic position, its tower commanding the southern approach to the city. It was important to the King's Men if they wanted to starve the Queen's Men out, and it was important to the Queen's Men for keeping a supply route to the city open. The Earl of Moray, the young king's Regent, was not entirely sure of Sir Archibald's loyalty – he may have vowed that he supported the king, but he had not, after all, fought actively for him. Moray wanted to keep Napier of Merchiston under his control.

Civil war was not Edinburgh's only trouble. In 1568 the scourge of the 'pestilence' took great toll on the population, and while Sir Archibald sent his children to his lands in the country, he himself was not allowed to leave. Those who lived in Merchiston Tower were in great peril from catching the disease, for it was the order of the Town Council that when a family was infected all the members had to leave their home, taking their goods and chattels with them, so that the house could be cleaned. The people were sent to the burgh muir, which was adjacent to the Napier lands. All round the walls of the estate lay the dead and dying. Infection was rife.

It is not known exactly when John came home, but domestic changes awaited him. He had a new stepmother, Elizabeth Mowbray of Barnbougall, a cousin of his father. The politics in this marriage were indeed confusing, because Elizabeth's family were Queen's Men, and her two younger sisters were so loyal to Mary, Queen of Scots that they joined her in England and shared her captivity until Mary was executed 15 years later.

In the midst of all the dangers of the plague and civil war, John decided to get married. The first of his marriage contracts was drawn up in 1571. Aged 21, he was contracted to marry Elizabeth Stirling of Keir, whose father, Sir James, had been a judge with Sir Archibald. The contractual arrangements were prolonged and precise. The groom's father was to receive a dowry of 3000 merks, and the groom was invested by his father with the baronies of Edinbellie-Napier and Merchiston. This meant that Napier became 'Fear' of Merchiston, because he had been invested with the fee, or title, of his paternal barony while his father was still alive. After this arrangement he often signed his name as 'Jhone Neper, Fear of Merchiston'. On 2 April 1572 a final deed was signed by John and Elizabeth. But in the disturbed times of the day there could be no wedding yet.

Within a month of signing these contracts Merchiston Tower was being besieged by the Queen's Men, anxious to quell the opposition and, of course, to get food into the city. Forces of the King's Men rushed to the rescue from Leith, and although they defeated the attackers on this occasion this was not the end of the battle around Merchiston. A concentrated attack by the Queen's Men was mounted on 10 June 1572, carefully timed for a day when the King's Men were busy besieging another castle. Cannon balls battered the tower for two hours and did a great deal of damage. For two weeks the battle raged back and forth until a truce, albeit a temporary one, was reached.

It is hardly likely that John was in the castle during all of this – his family had estates at Lennox and Menteith where he could have gone. Nevertheless, the wedding arrangements were proceeding. By October 1572 John and Elizabeth were granted a royal charter assigning them joint ownership of Edinbellie and Gartness in Stirlingshire. John, in addition, was given 'the lands of Merchiston with its tower and Pultrielands; half the lands of Ardewnan, etc. with the house of Barnisddale; the third of the lands of Calziemuck; and the lands of Auchinlesh'. But although he had lands, he did not necessarily have a large income, for his father and stepmother kept the life-rents of these estates. John and Elizabeth were finally married in 1573.

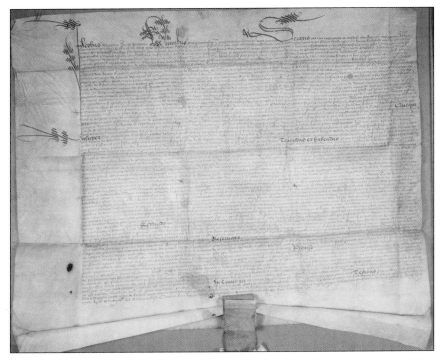

After his marriage contract was signed, John became 'Fear of Merchiston', a title he frequently used. (Courtesy of the National Archives of Scotland. Ref. GD430/135/1/1)

17

A COUNTRY LAIRD
OR A SORCERER?

AFTER his wedding Napier divided his time between Merchiston Castle and the estate at Gartness in Stirlingshire, where he and Elizabeth may have gone to enjoy a little peace. His father's second marriage was fruitful – Elizabeth Mowbray gave him nine children, of whom five survived, and this large family probably based themselves at Merchiston. As Sir Archibald was only 35 years old when he remarried, his children by Elizabeth Moubray were roughly of the same age as John's own children, resulting in John being more of an uncle to them, rather than a half-brother.

A son, Archibald, was born to Elizabeth and John at Gartness in 1576, and then there came a daughter, Jane. But this family happiness was to be short-lived, for Elizabeth died in 1579. She was barely 27 years old.

In contrast to the hurly-burly and often perilous life at Merchiston in the capital city, Gartness was a comparatively safe haven in the country. The family lived in Gartness Castle on the Drumquhassle Estate. The Great Seal of Scotland, 1424–1513, has an entry for 22 February 1494: 'Archibald Naper of Merchiston terras et Molendinum de Gartnes' (the lands and mill of Gartness); proving that the lands of Gartness had been in the Napier family for nearly a century. A date stone of 1574 from Gartness Castle, now set into the gable-end of a building that was originally a nearby mill, suggests that John Napier extended the castle when he got married, or even built a new one.

The castle stood on the banks of the River Endrick near Drymen and about two miles from Killearn. There are no signs of it left now, but it is marked on Blaeu's map of 1654, together with two mills, one a waulk mill and the other a corn mill.

Surrounded by sloping fields, and with Loch Lomond not far away, this was an ideal place to bring up a large family, and John proceeded to do just that. A few years after Elizabeth's death he married Agnes, the daughter of Sir James Chisholm of Cromix, and Elizabeth's second cousin. They had five sons and five daughters, bringing Napier's family up to twelve. Merchiston Castle is really quite a small tower – it is difficult to imagine how they all fitted in if the family sojourned to Edinburgh *en masse*.

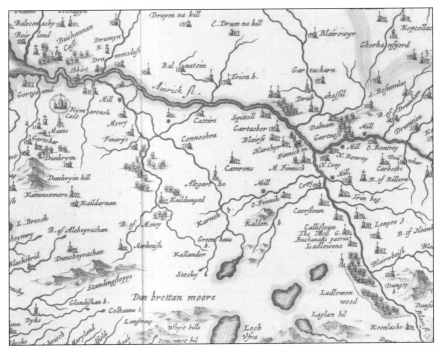

There are no signs of Napier's castle at Gartness now, but it is marked on Blaeu's Atlas of 1654. (Reproduced by permission of the Trustees of the National Library of Scotland)

It is alleged by several writers that at about this time, when Napier was beginning his great works, he had the reputation of being a warlock. Certain goings-on at Fast Castle on the Berwickshire coast in 1594 contributed to this hearsay. In addition at Gartness, according to folklore, he was apparently startling the local people by walking about at night in his nightgown and cap. Two centuries later in the 1790s this oral history was still alive and it was repeated by the Rev. David Ure in his section on the Parish of Killearn in the first *Statistical Account of Scotland*. He says:

> *This, with some things which to the vulgar appeared rather odd, fixed on him the character of a warlock. It was firmly believed, and currently reported, that he was in compact with the Devil; and that the time he spent in study was spent in learning the black art, and holding conversations with Old Nick.*

Biographers also report that it was not only at Gartness Napier had the reputation of being a warlock. Oral tradition had it that at Merchiston his very appearance aroused suspicion – he had a beard, and wore a black gown and a cowl. (However John Knox also had a beard, wore a black gown and a cowl – was he also a warlock? Those were simply the garments of the studious men of those times.) The stories grew. Napier, they said, had as a pet a black cock; surely this was because he dealt with the black arts! The reality was that Napier had taken over from his father the office of King's Poulterer – their lands included the 'pultrie landis' which were at the village of Dene near Edinburgh. The King's Poulterer had to give the sovereign a gift of poultry every year – perhaps one year Napier rather fancied a black cock in the basket and, saving it from the royal table, kept it as a pet.

One amusing tale about this pet was that he used it to trap a thief in the household. He told his servants that his bird could tell honesty from dishonesty, and would crow when a thief stroked its neck. He then sprinkled soot all over the cockerel, tied it up in a darkened room, and instructed all his servants to go in one by one and stroke the bird. The thief was soon found out, for he was afraid to stroke it, and was the only one to come out with clean, but guilty, hands.

More sorcery at Merchiston was also suspected when Napier had an argument with his neighbour, the Laird Roslin, whose pigeons were landing on Merchiston fields in large flocks and eating the grain. Napier said he would get the better of them. Roslin scoffed. Was it sorcery, the household and neighbours thought, that made the pigeons the next day reel about on the ground, unable to fly away from Napier's servants' grasping hands? Not a bit of it. Napier had soaked peas in wine and spread them all over the field. The pigeons loved the peas, but drunken pigeons cannot fly.

The affair of Fast Castle, however, was a more serious business and, in those days of witch-hunts and superstition, one which might well have landed Napier before the Council accused of witchcraft. (It must be remembered that in the sixteenth century the study of alchemy and the occult was as accepted as the study of physics and chemistry today, but the difficulty in Napier's time was treading the very fine line which was drawn between respectable research and dangerous black magic.)

In a rather bizarre fashion Napier got himself involved in a search for 'a soum of monie and poiss' (a hoard of treasure) that was believed to be 'heid and hurdit up secritlie' in Fast Castle in Berwickshire, and his partner in this venture was a very dubious character called Robert Logan of Restalrig, who had just been outlawed for sending his servants out to commit highway robbery. Logan owned Fast Castle, and in July 1594 he and Napier drew up a contract. It is written in Napier's own handwriting and signed by both men, but not witnessed by anyone. The whole affair is so extraordinary, and out of character for Napier, that it is worth looking at the contract in full (see pages 22–3):

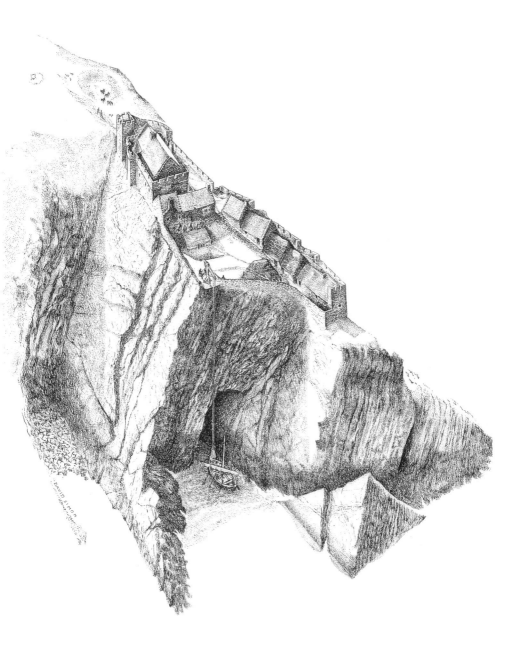

Fast Castle, standing high on its craggy promontory on the Berwickshire coast, could be reached by boat in the secrecy of the night. (Reconstruction of Fast Castle reproduced by permission of David Simon)

Contract Merchiston & Restalrik

At Edinbruch, Julij, yeir of God 1594 – It is apointit, contractit and agreit, betwix the personis ondirwrettin; that is to say, Robert Logane of Restalrige on the ane pairt, and Jhone Neper, fear of Merchiston, on the uther pairt, in maner, forme, and effect as folowis: – To wit, forsamekle as ther is dywerss ald reportis motiffis and appirancis, that thair suld be within the said Robertis dwellinge place of Fastcastell a soum of monie and poiss, heid and hurdit up secritlie, quilk as yit is on fund by ony man. The said Jhone sall do his utter and exact diligens to serche and sik out, and be al craft and ingyne that he dow, to tempt, trye, and find out the sam, and be the grace of God, ather sall find the sam, or than mak it suit that na sik thing hes been thair; sa far as his utter trawell diligens and ingyne may reach. For the quilk the said Robert sall giff, as be the tenour heirot, giffiis and grantis unto the said Jhone the just third pairt of quhatsoewir poiss or heid treasour the said Jhone sall find, or beis fund be his moyan and ingyn, within or abut the said place of Falscastell, and that to be pairtit be just wecht and balance, betwix thaim but only fraud, stryff, debait, and contention, on sik ,manner as the said Robert sall heff the just twa partis, and the said Jhone the just third pairt thpereof upone thair fayth, truth, and consciens. And for the said Jhonis suir return and saiff bakcumming tharwith to Edinbruch, on beand spulzeit [deprived] of his said thrid pairt, or utherways hairmit in body, or geir, the said Robert sall mak the said Jhone saiff convoy, and accumpanie him saifflie in maner forsaid bak to Edinburgh, quher the said Jhone, beand saiflie returnit, sall, in presens of the said Robert, cancell and destroy this present contract, as a lull discherg of ather of thair pailrtis honestlie satisfiet and performit to utheris; and ordanis that na uther discherge heirof but the destroying of this present contract sal be of ony awaill, forse, or effect. And incaiss the said Jhone sal find na poiss to be thair eftir all tryall and utter diligens tane; he referris the satisfactione of his trawell and painis to the discretione of the said Robert – In witnes of thir presens, and of all honestie, fideletie, fayth, and uprycht doing to be observit and keipit be bayth and saidis pairtis to uther, thei heff subscrywit thir presentis with thair handis at Edinbruch, day and yeir forsaid.

Robert Logane
of Restalrige
Jhone Neper, Fear of Merchistoun

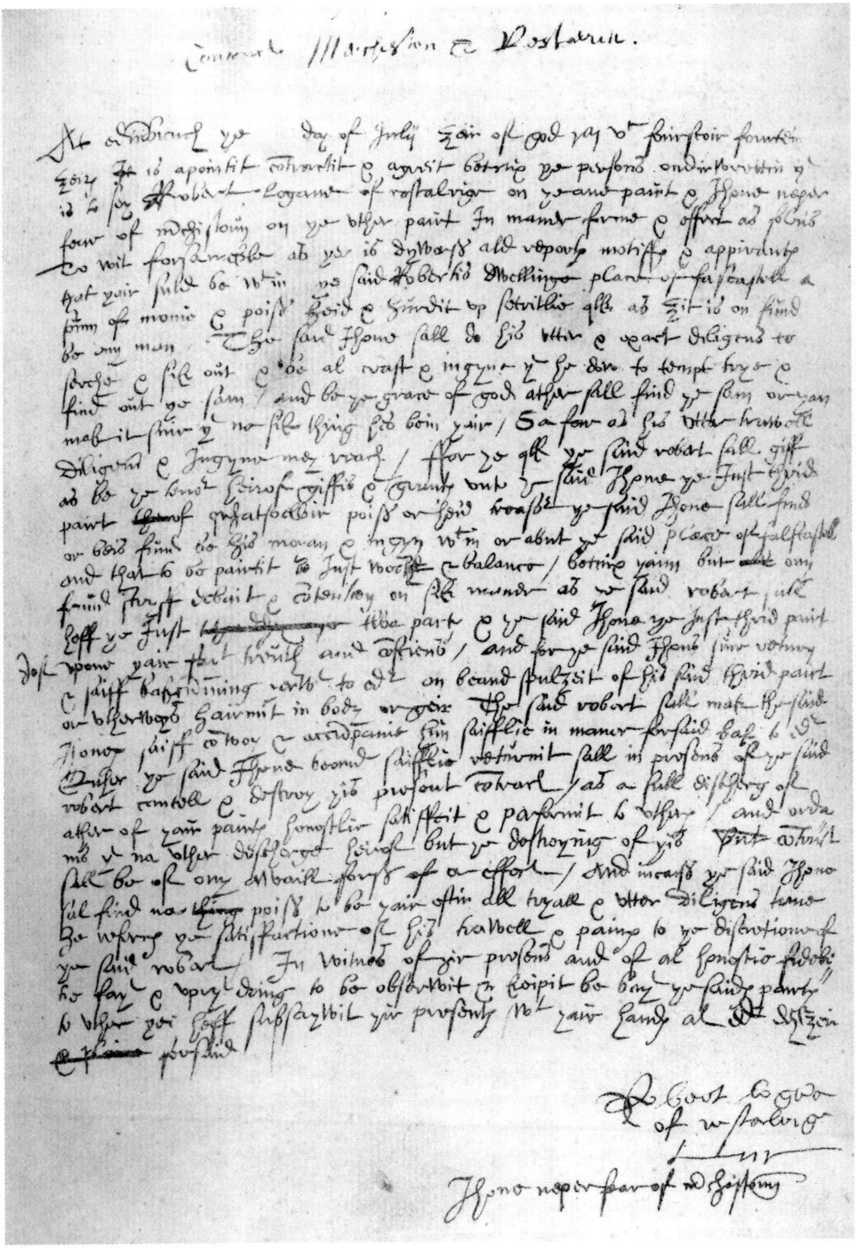

Contract Marchistoun & Restalrig.

At Edinburgh ye day of July ye zeir of god jaj vc fourscoir fourten
zeiris It is apointit contractit & agreit betuix ye persons vnderwrittin yt
is to say Robert Logane of restalrig on ye ane pairt & Jhone neper
fear of merchistoun on ye vther pairt In maner forme & effect as folowis
To wit forasmekle as yr is dyvers ald reports motiffs & appirances
yat yair suld be wtin ye said Robertis dwelling place of fastcastell a
soum of monie & poiss hid & hurdit vp secretlie qlk as zit is on fund
be ony man. The said Jhone sall do his vtter & exact diligens to
serche & seik out & be al craft & ingyne yt he dow to tempt try &
find out ye sam / and be ye grace of god ather sall find ye sam or yan
mak it suir yt no sic thing hes bein yair / Sa far as his vtter travell
diligens & ingyne may reach / ffor ye qlk ye said robart sall giff
as be ye tenor heirof giffis & grants vnto ye said Jhone ye just third
pairt of quhatsoevir poiss or hid treasr ye said Jhone sall find
or beis fund be his moyan & ingyne wtin or about ye said place of fastcastell
and that to be pairtit be just weght & balance / betuix yaim but ony
fraud strif debait & contention on sic maner as ye said robart sall
haff ye just twa part & ye said Jhone ye just third pairt
dost yair fait trewth and otheris / and for ye said Jhones sure returning
& saiff hamcuming to ed. on beand spulzeit of his said third pairt
or vtherwayis harmit in body or geir The said robart sall mak the said
Jhone saiff convoy & accumpanie him saiflie in maner forsaid bak to ed.
Quher ye said Jhone beand saiflie returnit sall in presens of ye said
robart cancell & destroy yis present contract as a full discharg of
ather of yair pairts honestlie satisfeit & performit to vther / and ordainis
yt na vther discharge heirof but ye destroying of yis contract
sall be of ony avail force or effect / And incais ye said Jhone
sal find na poiss to be yair efter all tryall & vtter diligens taine
he referris ye satisfactioun of his travell & pains to ye discretioun of
ye said robart / In witnes of yir presents and of al honestie fidelitie
to fayl & upryt dealing to be observit & keipit be bayth ye saids pairtys
to vther yai haff subscrivit yir presentis wt yair hands at ed. ye zeir
presaid

Robert Logane of restalrig

Jhone neper fear of merchistoun

(Reproduced by permission of the Trustees of the National Library of Scotland)

Therefore, if no treasure was found, Napier undertook to assure Logan that 'no such thing had been there'. If Napier was successful in locating any treasure, however, he was to get a third of it and be escorted back to Edinburgh with his share by Logan himself – an extremely naïve agreement on Napier's part when, it surely has to be assumed, he knew he was dealing with a man who had just been outlawed for organising highway robbery. Once home at Merchiston, both men had to witness the destruction of the contract, signifying that the terms of it had been fulfilled. Napier was to get some recompense for his efforts if no treasure was found. As the contract survived in the Napier family papers, clearly its terms had not been carried out.

Over the centuries writers have propounded theories about the rumoured existence of hidden gold at Fast Castle. Standing high on its craggy promontory on the Berwickshire coast, it could be reached by boat in the secrecy of the night, and there are caves beneath it. It was an excellent place to hide treasure from enemies. One suggestion is that when the Order of the Templars was brutally suppressed by Pope Clement V in 1312, survivors fled from France to Scotland, taking their gold with them and finding a safe, convenient landing beach at Fast Castle. Here was an ideal place to hide their considerable treasure.

Then there is the case of the missing ransom money that was being conveyed south in 1429 to King Henry VI of England as part of the price King James I of Scotland had to pay for his release from captivity. When James Colstoun and his guard set off on the Tuesday following the feast of Pentecost in the year 1429, bearing 2000 merks to be delivered to the English king, he and his men were set upon and robbed of all they possessed. The attack, which is said to have been instigated, or even undertaken, by William Drax, the Prior of Coldingham and an accomplice, was near Fast Castle, and it was rumoured that the 2000 merks were hidden there.

Another theory, that of hidden Spanish gold, seems to be more plausible, especially in the light of Napier's intervention. In the aftermath of the threatened invasion of the Spanish Armada in 1588, both England and Scotland were for many years still fearful of another attack from Spain. Plots were hatched everywhere. In 1593 the Scottish Catholic earls, Gordon, Angus, Errol and Huntly, had signed blank pieces of paper which were to be delivered to King Philip of Spain with the invitation that he make a list on them of his conditions for sending support for a Catholic uprising in Scotland. The papers were discovered in the possession of the luckless courier George Kerr, and what became known as 'the affair of the Spanish Blanks' was bruited all over town.

In 1597 Kerr, who had escaped from captivity to Calais, was bold enough to return to Scotland, with the plan that he was 'minding to land at Haymouth

[Eyemouth] or Falscasell [Fast Castle] which be not far from Berwick'. Clearly he either knew Robert Logan of Fast Castle, or knew the terrain very well, and landed successfully – was he on a mission to remove gold from Fast Castle so that it could help fund an uprising in Scotland?

From his early days at St Andrews, Napier was a committed Protestant. If rumour reached him that Spanish gold was hidden at Fast Castle to be used to overthrow Protestantism, it would be natural for him to do all he could to uncover it and prevent its use for this purpose. Indeed, so real was his fear of invasion, that he was already busy at Merchiston Tower inventing amazing machines to repel it (see page 31).

Religion or politics may have been the reason for the Fast Castle contract, but there need not have been anything sinister about the contract itself. There was gold in Scotland – it had been mined for many years. In the reign of King James V, 300 men worked the seams, and miners even came from Germany to profitable shafts in Clydesdale. In 1582 when Sir Archibald Napier, John's father, had been made Master of the Mint, his responsibilities for mines and minerals were real ones. Sir Archibald himself was said to be skilled at detecting gold, and to have found it in the Pentland Hills. He was to be given the title of 'Generall of his Hienes Cunzie-House' ('the king's counting-house') and round the family dining-room table at Merchiston it would be perfectly understandable if the techniques of finding metals were discussed.

Divining with dowsing rods had been practised since the Middle Ages, and it is possible to feel pulses in the hazel twig, even through stone. Perhaps both father and son were known to be good at it. Napier, who had after all drafted out the Fast Castle contract, may even have instigated the idea for looking for gold at the castle, feeling that it was his duty to use his skills to prevent a Catholic uprising.

In whatever way he intended to go about his search, however, he would not have contemplated even letting it be thought that he was using sorcery. Consider the reign in which he lived. He was a man of James VI, who believed that it was his God-given duty to hunt down every witch and warlock in the land, and this he did with a relish that was sadistic, illogical and unrelenting. He personally supervised the unspeakably cruel 'tests' that were inflicted on terrified young girls and women accused of witchcraft. No one was free from suspicion, and rank did not protect anyone. In 1569 even the Lord Lyon King of Arms, William Stewart, was burnt at the stake in St Andrews, accused of sorcery; and the Earl of Bothwell, implicated in the case of the North Berwick witches who were supposed to have raised a storm which endangered the king's life when he was at sea, only avoided a similar fate by escaping from prison. In addition an accusation of witchcraft was a good way of getting rid of enemies. No one would risk it.

John Napier had personal, even critical, dealings with James VI in Scotland, but if one whiff of suspicion had fallen upon him for being a warlock he would not have stood a chance with his sovereign. In his day Napier was probably thought of as rather eccentric, but the rumours of his sorcery must surely belong to later years.

There is still a mystery, however, about the Fast Castle affair. Did Napier ever go to the castle? Did he suddenly think it was too dangerous, or did he have word that the Spanish gold had been secreted away? The contract was not destroyed so it was not fulfilled, but certainly Napier was left angry. In 1596, two years later, when he was making a land contract at Gartness, it was expressly stated that no one of the name of Logan would be allowed to farm the land.

As for the stories of the treasure? Excavations at Fast Castle by the Edinburgh Archaeological Field Society from 1971–86 uncovered no gold.

WEAPONS AGAINST
THE SPANIARDS

BY 1594, when Napier drew up the Fast Castle contract, the word 'logarithm' had not yet entered the English language. Doubtless by now the idea of doing research in mathematics had come into Napier's mind. Fascinated by figures, he was reasoning that there must be a short-cut method of doing long division and multiplication sums instead of the way merchants, navigators and astronomers had to use presently, and certainly he must have been spending time covering pages and pages with exploratory figures to this end.

He had left the church where his ancestors had worshipped, St Giles' in Edinburgh, and had become a member of his parish church, St Cuthbert's. He was made an elder there, from which it must be assumed that he attended regularly and did not spend long stretches of his time at Gartness. In 1588 the Presbytery of Edinburgh appointed him Commissioner to the General

In John's time as an elder at St Cuthbert's Parish Church, the Nor' Loch lapped not far from the building. (Courtesy of St Cuthbert's Church)

Assembly of the Church of Scotland. This was the year of the setting out of the Spanish Armada, whose purpose was to conquer England and Scotland, and to subjugate both these Protestant countries to Catholic Spain. While there was still support in the north and the south-west for Roman Catholicism, the people in the Reformed Church were much alarmed.

James Melvill, the contemporary diarist, describing the scene in the General Assembly of the Church of Scotland, wrote: 'Terrible was the feir; persing [piercing] were the preachings; ernest, zealus and fervent war the prayers; sounding war the siches [sighs] and sobbes; and abounding war the tears ....' It was thought that the Spanish might land at Dunbar, St Andrews, Aberdeen or Cromarty.

Napier did not sit back in this crisis. His inventive mind turned to thinking about how best to defend Scotland in the face of a Catholic invasion and what kind of weapons would help. Action on the theological front was also required, he felt. As he himself stated, ever since his time at St Andrews he had wanted to write on the Apocalypse of the *Whole Revelation of Saint John*, and he now proceeded to do this, a dissertation which he saw in terms of an assault on the Roman Catholic religion and a defence of Protestantism. The Spaniards had to be vanquished on all fronts.

As it was, in 1588 the Spanish Armada met with defeat at the hands of the English ships, but the fear of another invasion attempt did not fade away. Napier kept working at his book, and *A Plaine Discovery of the whole Revelation of Saint John* was published in 1593. It was an instant success. This very earnest piece of religious writing was published a year before Napier signed the Fast Castle contract – it seems hardly likely that he was proposing to use black magic to locate gold when his Christian faith was so obviously committed.

In addition, that same year Napier was appointed by a convention to be a member of a delegation to meet the king. Their message was uncompromising and fearless. They were to 'declare freely to his majesty the mind and resolution of all his godly and faithful subjects within the province, that they were ready to give their lives rather than suffer the same to be polluted with idolatry, and overrun with bloody Papists'.

The Catholic earls and others implicated in the affair of the Spanish Blanks were to have no mercy. They had

> ... *by their idolatry, heresy, blasphemy, apostacy, perjury, and professed emnity against the kirk and true religion of Jesus Christ within his realm, ipso facto cut themselves off from Christ and his kirk, and so become most worthy to be declared excommunicated, and cut off from the fellowship of Christ and his kirk, and to be given over to the hands of Satan, whose slaves they were, that they may learn, if it so please God, not to blaspheme Christ of his Gospel.* [One of those

unfortunate 'heretics' was Sir James Chisholm, his own father-in-law, but Napier did not shrink from what he thought was his duty.]

The king, adept at handling the various factions in his realm, demurred, procrastinated and bargained. The 'heretic' earls armed themselves near Perth: some of the Protestant barons gathered together an army to face them. The king, however, once again brought his diplomacy to bear – a battle was avoided and another convention arranged. Napier clearly became impatient with this situation and boldly wrote a letter to the king, which he sent as a preface to his *Plaine Discovery of the whole Revelation of Saint John*. He did not mince his words:

The *Plaine Discovery* is to modern eyes a curious mixture of bigotry, scholarship and humility. (Plate from the *Napier Memorial Volume*, NMS Library)

> *... for verily and in trueth, such is the injury of this our present time, against both the Church of God and your Majestie's true lieges, that religion is despised, and justice utterly neglected: for what by Atheists, Papists and cold professors, the religion of god is mocked in all estates. Againe, for partialities, prolixitie, dearth, and deceitfulnes of lawes, the poore perishe, the proud triumphe, and justice is nowhere to be found ....*
>
> *Therefore, Sir, let it be your Majestie's continuall study to reforme the universalle enormities of your country, and first to begin at your Majestie's owne house, familie and court, purge the same of all suspicion of Papists and Atheists or Newtrals, whereof the Revelation telleth that the number shall greatly increase in these latter daise.*

The *Plaine Discovery* itself is to modern eyes a curious mixture of bigotry, scholarship and humility. Glimpses of the mathematician also come through. The subject of the book, the biblical Apocalypse attributed to the apostle St John, is so obscure that even Calvin had admitted that he could not understand it. Basically, it is a set of prophecies with timescales, and Napier interpreted them as proof that the Pope was Antichrist and that only the Reformers were righteous. From the Revelation, Napier argued, it was possible to work out when the world would end.

Napier's decision to write the *Plaine Discovery* was not an easy one. He himself wrote of his difficulty. Clearly very strongly influenced at St Andrews by the sermons of Maister Christopher Goodman and his teachings on the Apocalypse, he claimed that he was 'moved in admiration against the blindness of Papists that could not more evidentlie see their seven hilled Citie of Rome, painted out there so lively by Saint John, as the Mother of all Spiritual whoredome'.

> *... thenceforth I determined with myself by the assistance of God's spirit to employ my study and diligence to search out the remanent mysteries of that holy booke (as to this houre praised by the Lord I have bin doing at all such times as convenientlie I might have occasion.)*

The 'Maister' Christopher Goodman who inspired young John so greatly was an Englishman who had met John Knox in Geneva and agreed with his ideas for the Reformation of the Church. After 1560 he took up a charge in St Andrews as a Reformed minister, and from his pulpit he robustly propounded his Calvinistic views. It was acceptable, he said, for subjects to rebel against their sovereigns if circumstances demanded it. Goodman did not believe in the Divine Right of Kings and John Napier came to share this view.

In the sixteenth century there were no hard and fast boundaries between the study of scientific theories supported by facts and propositions put forward without benefit of logic, and Napier set out to find out from the *Whole Revelation of Saint John* when the world would end. He divided his book into two, the first having 38 Propositions, and the second having his commentaries on every verse in the Book of Revelation. The interesting point is that he saw this in mathematical terms. He calculated that the fulfilment of the Prophesies were as set out below.

The sound of the seventh Trumpet, or pouring out of the seventh Vial, began in 1541. This trumpet sound or Vial would last for 245 years – as they all had through the centuries – and therefore the seventh Trumpet would end in the year 1786. In his tenth Proposition he writes:

> *Not that I meane that that age, or yet the world shall continue so long, because it is said that, for the Elect's sake, the time shall be shortened; but I meane that if the world were to endure, that seventh Age should continue untill the yeare of Christ 1786.*

He states in his fourteenth Proposition that the Day of God's Judgement would be between 1688 and 1700. He concludes with firm resolution that the Pope is Antichrist: 'The whole work of Revelation concerneth most the discovery of the Antichristian and Papisticall Kingdome.'

Of course this was music to the ears of the Reformers all over Europe, and the book was immediately hailed as momentous. It would have been natural for Napier to have written it in Latin, but he himself was so enthused with his findings that he wanted to share it with all the people. It was published in English in 1593, and by 1645 there had been five editions. By 1607 there were three editions in Dutch and nine in French. Four German editions came out between 1611 and 1627. In Europe, Napier acquired considerable prestige as a theologian, and to the end of his days he thought this was his greatest work. Yet he had always been humble about it. In its preface he had written: 'I have not done herein perfectly as I would, yet zealously as I could.'

It is a measure of the diversity of Napier that while he was seeking inspiration to foretell the end of God's world in the *Plaine Discovery*, he was also concerning himself with inventing machines of war to protect not only his own country, but England too, from a second Spanish Armada. The Papists must be defeated at all costs. By 1596 Napier sent a list of his 'Secret Inventions' to the government in England. His contact was Anthony Bacon, and his letter to him survives:

Anno Domini 1596, the 7 of June, Secrett Inventionis, proffitabill and necessary to theis days for defence of this Iland, and withstanding of strangers, enemies of God's truth and religion.

First, the invention, proofe and perfect demonstration, geometricall and alegebricall, of a burning mirrour, which, receiving the dispersed beames of the sonne, doth reflex the same beames alltogether united and concurrting priselie [precisely] in one mathematicall point, in the which point most necessarelie it ingendreth fire, with an evident demonstration of their error who affirmeth this to be made a parabolik section. The use of this invention serveth for burning of the enemies shipps at whatsoever appointed distance.

Secondlie, the invention and sure demonstration of another mirrour which receiving the dispersed beams of any materiall fier or flame yealdeth allsoe the former effect, and serveth for the like use.

Thirdlie, the invention and visible demonstration of a piece of artillery, which, shott, passeth not linallie [in a straight line] through the enemie, destroying onlie those that stand on the random [line] thereot, and fra them forth flying idly, as utheris do: but passeth superficially, ranging abrode within the whole appointed place, and not departing furth of the place till it hath executed his whole strength, by destroying those that be within the boundes of the said place. The use hereof not onlie serveth greatlie against the armie of the enemy on land, but alsoe by sea it serveth to destroy, and cut downe, and [by] one shott the whole mastes and tackling of so many shippes as be within the appointed boundes, as well abried [abroad] as in large, so long as any strength at all remayneth.

Fourthlie, the invention of a round chariot of mettle made of the proofe of double muskett, which motion shall be by those that be within the same, more easie, more light, and more spedie by much than so manie armed men would be otherwayes. The use hereof as well, in moving, serveth to breake the array of the enemies battle and to make passage, as also in staying and abiding within the enemies battle, it serveth to destroy the environed enemy by continuall charge and shott of harquebush through small hoalles; the enemy in the meanetime being abased and altogether uncertaine what defence or pursuit to use against a moving mouth of mettle.

These inventiones, besides devises of sayling under the water, with divers other devises and stratagemes for harming of the enemyes, buy the grace of God and worke of expert craftesmen I hope to perform.

Jo. Neper, Fear of Merchistoun

So Napier claimed to have invented a tank, a submarine and an artillery piece capable of long-range bombardment.

It was later asserted in a tract by Sir Thomas Urquhart of Cromarty, published in 1652, that the field gun was tested in Scotland with astonishing results. He wrote:

He had the skill to frame an engine which, by vertue of some secret springs, inward resorts, with other implements and materials fit for the purpose, enclosed within the bowels thereof to clear a field of four miles circumference of all the living creatures exceeding a foot in height that should be found thereon, howsoever near they might be to one another: by which means he made it appear that he was able, with the help of this machine alone, to kill 30,000 Turks without the hazard of one Christian. Of this it is said that he gave proof upon a large plain in Scotland, to the destruction of a great many herds of cattle and flocks of sheep, whereof some were half a mile distant from others on all sides and some a whole mile.

There seems to be some embroidery in this tale, for surely there would have been other reports of such a remarkable occurrence. The second Armada did not come, however, and Napier's inventions were never put to the real test, and indeed never got beyond the drawing board. In fact, before his death he destroyed his drawings, in spite of pressure to publish them. He felt that the danger of being overrun by Papists had passed and that already there were too many devices in existence for the overthrow of man … 'therefore seeing that the malice and rancor rooted in the heart of mankind will not suffer them to diminish, by any new conceit of his, the number of them should never be increased'.

Tradition in the Napier family has it that a tank-like machine was buried at Gartness on the instructions of Napier. This was recorded by his descendant, Mark Napier, in the nineteenth century. The legend lives on.

All the time that Napier was working away at his calculations for these inventions, however, and all the time that he was running his estates and dealing with their accounts, he was thinking that there must be an easier way to do the long division and multiplication sums involved. His next invention, which he named 'logarithms', was not to be buried at Gartness.

Napier's fertile mind also turned to improving the Archimedes Screw — a water pump. He was given a monopoly to produce his pumps by James VI on 30 January 1596. (Courtesy of the National Archives of Scotland. Ref. GD430/150)

LOGARITHMS –
THE QUANTUM LEAP

WHEN John Napier finalised his work on his greatest invention, logarithms, there was no Archimedes-style leaping out of the bath and shouting 'Eureka'. Indeed, there was probably no great defining moment at all for him. He had plodded away quietly for at least 20 years on his mathematical research, working out countless calculations, but he regarded this rather as a hobby. His priorities had been studying for his theological publication, running his estates, and honouring his kirk commitments.

In the end, when news was beginning to seep out of Merchiston Tower that he had evolved a way of simplifying large calculations by the use of sets of tables, Napier realised that his ideas might be pirated and he decided to publish in 1614. His discovery had to have a name, and he chose *Mirifici Logarithmorum Canonis Descriptio*.

The entire work is in Latin, the common tongue among educated people in Europe, but Napier made up a name for his invention with Greek roots. *Logos* is the Greek for ratio or reckoning; *arithmos* is Greek for number. Napier wanted there to be no mistake about the authorship of the *Mirifici Logarithmorum*. On the richly decorated title page he put:

> *Authore ac Inventore,* IOANNE NEPERO,
> *Barone Merchistonii, &c. Scoto.*

The work appeared as a quarto book of 57 pages of explanations and 90 pages of tables.

In the field of mathematics, Napier's discovery was momentous. Although the navigators on the great voyages now taking place had quadrants for their charts instead of the astrolabe which Columbus had used, they still had to do enormous, cumbersome, error-prone calculations to find out exactly where they were. The invention of logarithms released the navigators from all this. For them and for the architects, merchants, bankers, and most of all for the astronomers, life was changed completely – and immediately. When Kepler, the imperial mathematician at Prague in 1601, calculated the orbit of the planet Mars without the benefit of logarithms, it took him four years.

Putti, scrolls and fruit richly decorate the title page of a book which was to herald a momentous mathematic advance.
(Plate from the *Napier Memorial Volume*, NMS Library)

The modern computer, which has evolved from Napier's invention, can take seconds to do the same task.

The extraordinary point about Napier's discovery was that it was achieved far away from scientific exploration in mainstream Europe. At a congress held in Edinburgh to mark the 300th anniversary of the publication of logarithms, Lord Moulton said:

> *No previous work had led up to it, nothing had foreshadowed it or heralded its arrival. It stands isolated, breaking upon human thought abruptly, without borrowing from the works of other intellects or following known lines of mathematical thought.*

To modern thinking the land in which logarithms were born was primitive and bigoted. In Edinburgh, while Napier rode or walked the streets, he had to be careful to duck quickly at the screech 'gardeyloo', which meant that garbage and night-soil were being heaved out of upper windows in the tall tenements of the Lawnmarket and the High Street, down on to the closes and wynds below. Frequently pigs were kept on the ground floor of the houses, and people, when they climbed the outside stairs to the houses up above, had to avoid the animals rootling in the rotting middens. If Napier was unwise enough to drink from a well in the street, the chances were high that it was sunk in disease-ridden soil. Pestilence reared its ugly head often, and the well-born were not exempt.

The leaders of religion – Roman Catholic priests before the Reformation and Protestant ministers after it – constantly strove to have a stranglehold on the people, with the power to suppress individual thought in many fields. After 1560, sexual offences were considered to be extremely heinous by the Presbyterians, and even men's dress was dictated – hair had to be short and sombre colours should be worn. In Napier's own church, St Cuthbert's, a pillar for the humiliation of delinquents was introduced in 1590. Everywhere the sentence of excommunication was forever round the corner. New discoveries were treated with suspicion, just as they had been before the Reformation – they might challenge the accepted tenets of the day.

Yet Scotland's creative minds were not snuffed out. Scotland was not a cultural desert. In Edinburgh, by 1550 the beautiful crown steeple of St Giles' Kirk had risen above all the filth and smells of the High Street. Long, narrow gardens behind the tall tenements yielded not only flowers, but vegetables and fruit. The College of Surgeons of Edinburgh had been established and received its charter from James IV, 45 years before Napier was born. The College of Justice had been founded, and by 1582 Scotland, with its tiny population, had four universities compared to England's two, and this was to remain so for nearly 300 years.

As early as the thirteenth century fine carvings had adorned Holyrood Abbey. The poetry of William Dunbar, born in the fifteenth century, is among Scotland's finest. Gavin Douglas translated Virgil's *Aeneid* into Scots in 1513 – the first version of a Latin poet in the vernacular. Sir David Lyndsay of the Mount had Scottish playgoers laughing and cheering in 1540 at his *Ane Satyre of the Thrie Estaitis*. The composer, Robert Carver, a canon at Scone, had moved the worshippers with his Masses, noted for his free use of counterpoint. One of his surviving motets is written for 19 voice parts. Architects and builders had the skill to raise houses six storeys high, or higher. The Great Tenement in Parliament Square was 14 storeys high. The religious and heraldic paintings of the time compared favourably with those in Europe. In particular, the 'Stirling Heads', the oak roundels carved to decorate a ceiling in Stirling Castle around 1540, were an outstanding example of the craftsmen's skill.

However, contrary to common belief, the Reformation did not kill off all enjoyment. For instance, in 1590 Edinburgh's Town Council invited the great and the good to the large mansion built by Baillie McMorran in Riddle's Court for a lavish banquet given in honour of James VI and his bride, Anne of Denmark. For such occasions, and for the tables of the wealthy, the Scottish gardeners, making skilful use of walled gardens, were growing ambitious varieties of vegetables and fruit. The diners may not have been using forks yet, but by the seventeenth century, many of them were having a choice of cabbage, cauliflower, onions, leeks, shallots, celery, asparagus, parsnips, carrots, turnips, beetroot and fennel. In the fruit bowls were apples, pears, cherries, raspberries, strawberries, gooseberries, plums, peaches and even apricots. The flowerbeds were bright with carnations, anemones, ranunculus, violets and many other blooms, and on the big estates the gardens were beginning to be laid out in elaborate, formal designs.

John Knox had died before Napier had begun any serious work on the logarithms, but with the Reformation in Scotland came the Presbyterian work ethic. Since the days of James IV education had been prized. Talent there was in abundance. In the field of mathematics, Napier saw that there was a necessity to find shortcuts to doing large calculations. He did not seem to need the stimulus of meeting mathematicians abroad to help him to get on with his search for these shortcuts. He found it quite natural to sit at his desk in Merchiston Castle, pull his paper towards him, take up his quill and work away at his calculations.

When *Mirifici Logarithmorum Canonis Descriptio* was published in 1614, the East India Company, immediately seeing its potential not only for its merchants but for its navigators, engaged a Cambridge mathematician, Edward Wright, to translate it from the original Latin into English. This was printed in 1616, after Napier had approved the translation.

The Preface is engagingly modest:

Seeing there is nothing (right well-beloved Students of the Mathematics) that is so troublesome to mathematical practice, nor that doth more molest and hinder calculations, than the multiplications, divisions, square and cubical extractions of great numbers, which besides the tedious expense of time are for the most part subject to many slippery errors, I began therefore to consider in my mind by what certain and ready art I might remove these hindrances. And having thought upon many things to this purpose, I found at length some excellent brief rules to be treated of (perhaps) hereafter. But amongst all, none more profitable than this which together with the hard and tedious multiplications, divisions and extractions of roots, doth also cast away from the work itself even the very numbers themselves that are to be multiplied, divided and resolved into roots, and putteth other numbers in their place which perform as much as they can do, only by addition and subtraction, division by two or division by three. Which secret invention, being (as all other good things are) so much the better as it shall be the more common, I thought good heretofore to set forth in Latin for the public use of mathematicians.'

Napier goes on to explain that it was felt that the use of logarithms should also be available 'in our vulgar English tongue':

Therefore it may please you who are inclined to these studies to receive it from me and the translator with as much goodwill as we recommend it unto you. Fare ye well.

Just how did Napier manage to eradicate those 'slippery errors'? In his *Canon Mirificus* he did not reveal how he calculated his logarithms. He wrote that he wanted to show their use, rather than how he had arrived there:

The use and the profit of the thing being first conceived, the rest may please the more, being set forth hereafter, or else displease the less, being buried in silence. For I expect the judgment and censure of learned men hereupon, before the rest, rashly published, be exposed to the detraction of the envious.

Napier's own description of how the logarithms work is in straightforward terms. To him it must have seemed so simple.

The logarithms were listed in tables beside the natural numbers for easy conversion, and once the addition or subtraction of the logarithms was done, then the answers were referred to the *anti*logarithm table, and changed back into 'real' numbers again. Napier then progressed to using his logarithms for finding square roots and cubes by multiplication and division.

Consistently in his *Mirifici Logarithmorum Canonis Constructio* (published posthumously in 1619), Napier, in order to simplify the expression of figures, used his version of writing decimal fractions with a decimal point. It was Henry Briggs who named the digit before the point in a log as the *characteristic* and those after the point as the *mantissa*.

To do the sum, say, of 7464 x 243 in pre-Napierian times, it would be carried out as follows:

$$\begin{array}{r} 7464 \\ \times\ \underline{243} \\ 1492800 \\ 298560 \\ \underline{22392} \\ 1813752 \end{array}$$

Bewilderment in the classroom — a twenty-first-century Merchiston Castle schoolboy abandons his calculator briefly to grapple with logarithm tables. (Photo: David Stranock)

To do the same sum of 7464 x 243 using Napier's log tables, the method is as follows:

First, work out the characteristics of the numbers you wish to multiply. The characteristic is always one digit fewer than the number of digits. For example, the characteristic of 7464 is 3, and the characteristic of 243 is 2.

The mantissa is found by using log tables. A section is shown below. For 7464, locate the 74 row and the 6 column. This gives 0.8727. There remains the unit figure of 4 and for this you look further along the 74 row to the ADD columns, for 4. Down in the 74 row this becomes 2. This is added to the 0.8727 and becomes a mantissa of 0.8729. The complete logarithm of 7464 is therefore 3.8729. The same process is applied to 243, which gives a logarithm of 2.3856. Subsequently for greater accuracy five-, six- and seven-figure log tables would have been used.

| LOGARITHMS, BASE 10 | | | | | | | | | | | | | | ADD | | | | |
$\log_{10}$	0	1	2	3	4	5	6	7	8	9	1	2	3	4	5	6	7	8	9
70	0.8451	0.8457	0.8463	0.8470	0.8476	0.8482	0.8488	0.8494	0.8500	0.8506	1	1	2	2	3	4	4	5	6
71	0.8513	0.8519	0.8525	0.8531	0.8537	0.8543	0.8549	0.8555	0.8561	0.8567	1	1	2	2	3	4	4	5	5
72	0.8573	0.8579	0.8585	0.8591	0.8597	0.8603	0.8609	0.8615	0.8621	0.8627	1	1	2	2	3	4	4	5	5
73	0.8633	0.8639	0.8645	0.8651	0.8657	0.8663	0.8669	0.8675	0.8681	0.8686	1	1	2	2	3	4	4	5	5
74	0.8692	0.8698	0.8704	0.8710	0.8716	0.8722	0.8727	0.8733	0.8739	0.8745	1	1	2	2	3	4	4	5	5
75	0.8751	0.8756	0.8762	0.8768	0.8774	0.8779	0.8785	0.8791	0.8797	0.8802	1	1	2	2	3	3	4	5	5
76	0.8808	0.8814	0.8820	0.8825	0.8831	0.8837	0.8842	0.8848	0.8854	0.8859	1	1	2	2	3	3	4	5	5
77	0.8865	0.8871	0.8876	0.8882	0.8887	0.8893	0.8899	0.8904	0.8910	0.8915	1	1	2	2	3	3	4	4	5
78	0.8921	0.8927	0.8932	0.8938	0.8943	0.8949	0.8954	0.8960	0.8965	0.8971	1	1	2	2	3	3	4	4	5
79	0.8976	0.8982	0.8987	0.8993	0.8998	0.9004	0.9009	0.9015	0.9020	0.9025	1	1	2	2	3	3	4	4	5

JOHN NAPIER

Traditionally, the sum was set out as follows:

no.	log
7464	3.8729
x 243	2.3856 (*the logarithm figures are now added*)
	6.2585

Changing the 6.2585 under the log column back to an ordinary number requires antilogarithms.

Dealing with the mantissa of 0.2585 first, using the antilogarithm table below, locate the 0.25 row and then look along under 8. This gives 0.1811. For extra accuracy in the ADD section go to 5 (the unit figure) which down in the 0.25 row gives 2. This is added to the 0.1811, giving 0.1813.

ANTILOGARITHMS, 10 ^x   ADD

10 ^x	0	1	2	3	4	5	6	7	8	9	1	2	3	4	5	6	7	8	9
0.20	1585	1589	1592	1596	1600	1603	1607	1611	1614	1618	0	1	1	1	2	2	3	3	3
0.21	1622	1626	1629	1633	1637	1641	1644	1648	1652	1656	0	1	1	2	2	2	3	3	3
0.22	1660	1663	1667	1671	1675	1679	1683	1687	1690	1694	0	1	1	2	2	2	3	3	3
0.23	1698	1702	1706	1710	1714	1718	1722	1726	1730	1734	0	1	1	2	2	2	3	3	4
0.24	1738	1742	1746	1750	1754	1758	1762	1766	1770	1774	0	1	1	2	2	2	3	3	4
0.25	1778	1782	1786	1791	1795	1799	1803	1807	1811	1816	0	1	1	2	2	2	3	3	4
0.26	1820	1824	1828	1832	1837	1841	1845	1849	1854	1858	0	1	1	2	2	3	3	3	4
0.27	1862	1866	1871	1875	1879	1884	1888	1892	1897	1901	0	1	1	2	2	3	3	3	4
0.28	1905	1910	1914	1919	1923	1928	1932	1936	1941	1945	0	1	1	2	2	3	3	4	4
0.29	1950	1954	1959	1963	1968	1972	1977	1982	1986	1991	0	1	1	2	2	3	3	4	4

Turning to the characteristic of 6, an extra digit must now be *added,* so that in this case the final answer will have seven digits. The extra figures are made up by adding noughts. The answer therefore is 1,813,000.

no.	log
7464	3.8729
x 243	2.3856
1813000	6.2585

To *divide* 7464 by 243, the log of 243 is *subtracted* from the log of 7464, and derived from the antilogarithm tables in a similar way.

no.	log
7464	3.8729
÷ 243	2.3856 (*the logarithm figures are now subtracted*)
30.71	1.4873

40

The antilog tables give the conversion of the mantissa of 0.4873 as 3071.

ANTILOGARITHMS, 10^x															ADD			
10^x	0	1	2	3	4	5	6	7	8	9	1	2	3	4	5	6	7	8	9
0.47	2951	2958	2965	2972	2979	2985	2992	2999	3006	3013	1	1	2	3	3	4	5	6	6
0.48	3020	3027	3034	3041	3048	3055	3062	3069	3076	3083	1	1	2	3	4	4	5	6	6
0.49	3090	3097	3105	3112	3119	3126	3133	3141	3148	3155	1	1	2	3	4	4	5	6	6

To the characteristic an extra digit must be added, as before, for the number of digits in the answer. In this case, the characteristic of 1 means that out of 3071 the answer will have two digits: 3 and 0. The other figures of 7 and 1 become decimal fractions and are put after Napier's decimal point. The answer is therefore 30.71.

Using only four-figure logs, as in this instance, the answer is not as accurate as the one given by a modern calculator, but complete accuracy can be achieved with more detailed logarithms.

While calculating his logs, Napier was using the decimal fractions invented by Simon Stevinus of Belgium in 1585. (These are fractions of a number expressed by continuing ordinary decimal notation into negative powers of ten. One quarter is therefore written as 0.25 and one eighth as 0.125.) But Stevinus had not succeeded in devising a simple method of expressing his decimal fractions, and would, for instance, have written 123.456 as 1 2 3 ⓪ 4 ① 5 ② 6 ③. It was Napier who introduced the system of expressing decimal fractions by separating them from their integers by a point. While his tables of logs *per se* have been superseded by calculators, no one has yet found a better way of expressing decimal fractions than by using Napier's decimal point.

Napier dedicated his book on logarithms to Prince Charles, the future Charles I, and in this he wrote:

> *This new course of logarithms doth clean take away all the difficulty that hereto-fore hath been in mathematical calculations, and is so fitted to help the weakness of memory, that by means hereof it is easy to resolve more mathematical questions in one hour's space, than otherwise can be done in a day. And, therefore, this invention (I hope) will be so much the more acceptable to your Highness, as it yieldeth a more easy and speedy way of accompt. For what can be more delightful and more excellent in any kind of learning than to dispatch honourable and profound matters exactly, readily, and without loss of either time or labour?*

THE WORLD'S FIRST
POCKET CALCULATOR

NAPIER's discovery of logarithms was of such importance that it did not take long for news of it to travel. Among those immediately interested was Henry Briggs, Professor of Mathematics at Gresham College in London. On 10 March 1615 he wrote to Archbishop Usher in these words:

> *Napier, Lord of Merchiston, hath set my head and hands at work with his new and admirable logarithms. I hope to see him this summer if it please God, for I never saw a book which pleased me better, and made me more wonder.*

Briggs was as good as his word, and he bravely set forth on the four-day journey from London to Edinburgh the next summer. The English astrologer William Lilly, who almost certainly must have known Briggs, recounted to Elias Ashmole (the benefactor of the Ashmolean Museum in Oxford) the story of this famous meeting:

> *I will acquaint you with one memorable story, related unto me by John Mair, an excellent mathematician and geometrician …. He was servant to King James First and Charles First.*
>
> *When Merchiston first published his logarithms, Mr Briggs, then reader of the Astronomy lectures at Gresham College in London, was so surprised with admiration of them, that he would have no quietness in himself, until he had seen that noble person whose only invention they were. He acquaints John Marr, who went into Scotland before Mr. Briggs, purposely to be there when these two so learned persons should meet; Mr. Briggs appoints a certain day when to meet at Edinburgh, but failing thereof, Merchiston was fearful he could not come. It happened one day as John Marr and the Lord Napier were speaking of Mr. Briggs: 'Ah John,' saith Merchiston, 'Mr. Briggs will not now come.'*
>
> *At that very instant one knocks at the gate; John Marr hasted down and it proved to be Mr. Briggs to his great contentment. He brings Mr. Briggs up into My Lord's chamber, where almost one quarter of an hour was spent, each beholding the other with admiration before one word was spoken.*

'My Lord's Chamber' at Merchiston Castle where Henry Briggs first met John Napier. It is now part of Napier University. (Courtesy of Napier University, Edinburgh)

> *At last Mr. Briggs began: 'My Lord, I have undertaken this long journey purposely to see your person, and to know by what engine of wit or ingenuity you came first to think of this most excellent help until Astronomy, viz the logarithms: but My Lord, being by you found out, I wonder nobody else found it out before, when now being known as it appears so easy.' He was nobly entertained by the Lord Napier, and every summer after that during the Laird's being alive, this venerable man Mr. Briggs went purposely to Scotland to visit him.*

Briggs stayed for a month at Merchiston Castle, and the two mathematicians got down to work. Briggs suggested in a letter to Napier before his visit that there would be greater advantage if the logarithm tables were to the base 10, instead of to Napier's original base e. Napier had already realised this, but explained to Briggs that ill-health and other 'weighty reasons' had prevented him from calculating new tables. They did not initially agree on the precise system. Briggs felt that it would be more convenient, while the logarithm of the whole sine was still taken as zero, to take the logarithm of the tenth part of the sine as a power of ten. He had in fact already begun calculating tables on this basis. Napier, however, preferred that zero should be the logarithm not of the whole sine but of unit, while, as suggested by Briggs, the logarithm of the tenth part of the sine should be a power of ten.

Briggs readily agreed that Napier's method was the better one, and it was he, with Napier's whole-hearted approval, who worked out the tables of logarithms to the base 10, which are essentially the same as those on every scientific calculator today. (Napierian logarithms still feature on calculators:

the button 'ln' gives logarithms to the base *e* and they are used particularly in calculus; differentiation and integration.)

On the continent it was Johannes Kepler, the German astronomer, who first saw the enormous importance of Napier's logarithms. They were published there in 1617, in Benjamin Ursinus' *Cursus Mathematicus Practicus*. Kepler had cursorily glanced at them previously, but had been somewhat dismissive. They were, he said, the work of '*Scotus Baro cujus nomen mihi excidit*' (a 'Scottish baron whose name escapes me').

However, a closer look at the logarithm theory in Ursinus' book dramatically changed Kepler's lukewarm attitude to one of great enthusiasm. He used the logarithms when working on his *Ephemeris* and dedicated it to Napier. The unknown baron had become the 'illustrious baron'.

At home, in virtually every field, the logarithms became a working tool. For example John Reid, a Scottish gardener, described at length in a book published in 1683 how to design and measure out a formal garden using logarithms.

After the publication of the logarithms, Napier did not rest. He realised that it would be advantageous to have a means of simple calculation in a less unwieldy form and also one more easily understood by people without the education of the professionals who were using the logarithms. His inventive mind set to work again, and by 1617, the year after the English translation of the *Canon of Logarithms* had been printed, sets of Napier's 'Numbering Rods' had been made and were indeed, as he himself stated, 'in common use'. He decided that he had better claim his invention, and the *Rabdologiae*, as Napier called his book, was published. Napier once more looked to the Greek language for the name of his work – *rhab'dos* means rod and *logiae* means a collection. The text, however, was in Latin. 'Napier's Bones', as the rods were to become known worldwide, were born.

There were actually three inventions described in this book:

> For the sake of those who prefer to work with natural numbers as they stand, I have excogitated three other compendious modes of calculation, of which the first is by means of numbering rods, and these I have called Rabdologiae.
>
> Another by far the most expeditious of all for multiplication, and which on that account I have not inaptly called the Promptuary of Multiplication, is by means of little plates of metal disposed in a box. And lastly, a third method, namely Local Arithmetic, performed on a chess board.

Napier wrote in the dedication to Alexander Seton, Earl of Dunfermline:

> To the publication of this little work, concerning the mechanism and use of the rods, I was specially impelled, not merely by the fact that they are so approved of as to be already

RABDOLOGIÆ,
SEV NVMERATIONIS
PER VIRGULAS
LIBRI DVO:

Cum Appendice de expeditif-
fimo Mvltiplicationis
Promptvario.

Qvibus accessit & Arithmeticæ
Localis Liber vnvs.

Authore & Inventore Ioanne
Nepero, Barone Mer-
chistonii, &c.
Scoto.

EDINBVRGI,
Excudebat Andreas Hart, 1617.

Napier did not live to see the publication of the
Rabdologiae. (Courtesy of NMS Library)

almost in common use, but it also reached my ears that your kindness advised me to do so, lest they should be published in the name of another, and I be compelled to sing with Virgil, 'Hos ego versiculos feci' – 'T's I who wrote those little lines.'

Like the book on logarithms, the *Rabdologiae* was an immediate success. It was entered at the Stationers' Company in London in 1617 and shown at the Frankfurt Book Fair. It was translated into German in 1618, and Italian in 1623. The Latin edition was reprinted in Leyden in 1626 and a Dutch translation came out in the same year. Sadly, Napier did not live to experience this amazing reaction, for he died in April 1617, before the very first edition had even appeared in Edinburgh.

What Napier did when he invented his numbering rods was to enable not only the merchants, the bankers and the navigators, but also the man in the street, to do basic, every-day sums quickly by using the convenient rods, instead of laboriously working with inkpots, quills, and sheets and sheets of paper.

They were first nicknamed 'Napier's Bones' in 1617 by Thomas Bretnor, possibly because some earlier sets were made in ivory. The Earl of Dunfermline had a set made of silver. Soon there were various types, mostly of wood. Some had little cases which were richly decorated, and some were small enough to go into a pocket – the world's first pocket calculators.

Once mastered, the Bones were easy to operate. Each set, as in Napier's design, had at least ten four-sided rods, together with a multiplying rod with the numbers 1 to 9 stamped down one of its faces. To the ten rods were allocated the digits 0 to 9, and the relevant digit was put at the top. The rods were marked off in diagonals, as in the illustration (right).

A   B

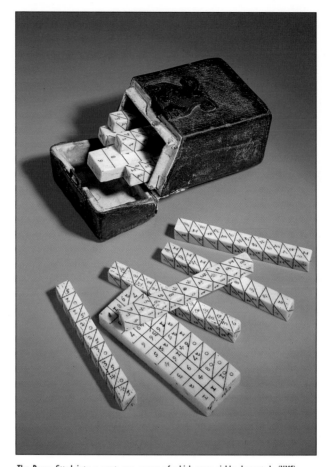

The Bones fitted into a neat case, many of which were richly decorated. (NMS)

The ten rods, of course, had 40 faces, and for allocating the digits to them Napier worked out a system based on figures which add up to nine. For instance, if one digit on the top of rod A (marked in red on the previous page) was 6, the digit on the opposite side was 3. Similarly, if the digit on rod B was 5, the parallel one on the other side was 4. The remaining two faces on each rod were likewise filled with digits which added up to nine – but there was no repetition of a pairing.

Therefore, the ten rods were marked on the top thus:

9/0 and 1/8	0/9 and 2/7	9/0 and 3/6	9/0 and 4/5
	1/8 and 2/7	1/8 and 3/6	1/8 and 4/5
		2/7 and 3/6	2/7 and 4/5
			3/6 and 4/5

Napier then placed the numbering rod (the multiplier), on the left of each rod in turn, and the figures to be put in the diagonals going downwards were simply the 'times' table of the top digit (in red) by each succeeding figure down the multiplier.

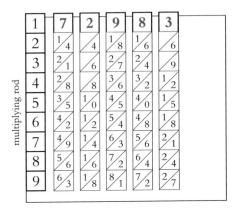

Using the rods to do a multiplication sum, say 72,983 x 9, the rods whose digits are 7, 2, 9, 8 and 3 are placed side by side, with the multiplying rod on their left.

The figures in the diagonals are read across in a straight line from the multiplying figure of 9, from left to right, and written down:

6/3 1/8 8/1 7/2 2/7

From *right to left*, the figures are then added:

6/3   1/8   8/1   7/2   2/7
= 6 + 4 + 16 + 8 + 4 + 7

The *tens* figures are now carried over to the left:

= 6   5   6   8   4   7

So the answer to 72,983 x 9 is 656,847.

If the multiplying figure is a two-digit one, say 93, then the sum is done first by 3 on the multiplying rod, then by 90, and the answers are added together. Division on the rods is a little more complicated but can be done, as can the extraction of square and cubic roots. When a rod is placed on a table, of course only one face is visible, and so for quick reference some rods have the digits of the hidden faces stamped on the foot of each face.

What Napier actually did with his Bones was to show that it is possible to multiply without knowing the multiplication tables.

The Promptuary was Napier's last mathematical discovery. (Courtesy of Museo Arqueológico Nacional, Madrid)

Napier's *Promptuary of Multiplication* almost disappeared into history, because for centuries it was believed that none had survived and there was only Napier's Latin description of it. However, recent research written up in *The Promptuary Papers*, published in 1988, uncovered a wealth of material. In this was reprinted a translation of Napier's Latin by William F Hawkins, a mathematician originally from London who retired to New Zealand.

Napier's thoughts on his invention were:

> *Although this* Promptuary *was discovered by me last of all, it deserves a better place than to be put last in the book. By using it, any multiplication, no matter how difficult or involved, can be done readily and with maximum speed.*
>
> *Divisions can also be done by its use, but they first have to be converted into multiplications, using either tables of sines, tangents and secants, or the tables in Book II, after I have explained how the* Promptuary *is constructed.*

From these instructions and diagrams, Hawkins in 1979 proceeded to build in the Engineering Workshops of Auckland University a replica of the Promptuary, and he wrote a full description of its complicated workings.

This was not the end of the story. A fellow Napier enthusiast, Erwin Tomash, was subsequently amazed and delighted to discover that there existed in the Museo Arqueológico in Madrid a highly decorated table-top cabinet, with doors that opened on to what seemed like drawers of numbered strips.

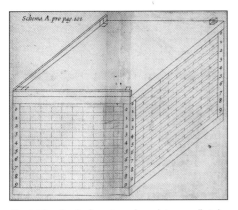

Schema A pro pag. 101.

The drawings for the Promptuary show what a complicated piece of machinery it was. It could be called the world's first calculating machine. (Courtesy of NMS Library)

No one in the museum knew exactly what it was, but to Tomash it immediately became clear. He had been alerted by the curators of the Adler Planetarium that there was a Napier instrument in Madrid, and he now found himself looking at the only surviving Promptuary from around Napier's time. Here was an example of the world's first calculating machine, the 'lightning calculator', as Napier called it.

'Promptuary' literally means 'storehouse', from *promptuarium* (Latin), and indeed this is just what Napier's was. It was an elaboration of the Bones, and consisted of two sets of flat strips, one of which was the *number* or *vertical* strip, the other the *aperture* or *horizontal* strip. For doing a multiplication sum, the figures to be multiplied were laid out vertically with number strips, and the multiplier horizontally with the aperture strips. The answer could then be read through the 'windows' formed by the vertical and horizontal strips.

The Madrid Promptuary even has a neat compartment containing a set of Napier's Bones that could be used on its own. Made of rosewood and inlaid with ivory, it was an ornamental piece of furniture which would grace any seventeenth-century study, but it was also a piece of equipment of superb technical sophistication for use by the mathematicians of the day.

The third device, named by Napier in his *Rabdologiae* as 'Local Arithmetic', required a chess board for its working. By moving counters on it, it was possible to do addition, subtraction, multiplication, division and the extraction of roots. Napier did not regard this last invention too seriously – it was more of an amusement. He put it in the *Rabdologiae*, he said, simply because he did not wish it to be buried in silence. It was, he thought, too small an invention to publish on its own.

Indeed, it did not stand the test of time. It is for the invention of logarithms and the Bones that Napier is known.

UP AMONG THE GREATS

THE nature of Napier's last illness is not exactly known. He had reached the age of 67 when he died on 4 April 1617, and by the standards of those disease-ridden times this was remarkable. Some writers claim that it was gout which caused his death – Napier does mention having gout in papers dated May 1613, concerning a dispute with the Grahams of Boquhopple, neighbours near Gartness. However, although gout may have been a contributing factor, it is doubtful that it actually caused his death.

He had been failing for some time, as he explained to Briggs. In the *Canonis Descriptio* – the logarithms – he says in the dedication, '*mihi jam morbis pene confecto*' ('that am now almost spent with sickness'), and in the '*Admonitio*' he speaks of his '*infirma valetudo*' ('poor state of health'). He is relieved that Briggs will take on the huge task of calculating the logarithms to the base 10 '*ob infirmam corporis nostra valetudinem*' ('on account of the infirmity of my bodily health').

However, his will was only drawn up three days before his death, when he no longer had the strength to hold his quill. His solicitor had to help him to sign the deed. In it he stated:

> … *being sick in bodie at the plesour of God, bot haill in mynd and spereit, and knawing nathing mair certane* [than] *death, and the tyme and manner thereof maist uncertane, and willing to dispose upon my wurldlie effairis, and to be dischairgit of the burding and cair thereof, so that at the plesour of Almichtie God I may be reddie to abyd his guid will and plesour quhen it sall pleis him to call me out of this transitorie lyfe.*

Six of his twelve children were still minors, so Agnes, Alexander, Elizabeth, William, Helen and Adam were to be looked after by his wife Agnes, 'my loving spous', and they were left a third of his estate. If Agnes remarried, however, his son Robert, who was the second son of his marriage to her, was to be their tutor and take responsibility for them.

Napier died at Merchiston Castle and was buried in his parish church,

The memorial tablet in St Cuthbert's Church is designed to echo the title page of the *Mirifici Logarithmorum*. (Courtesy of St Cuthbert's Church)

St Cuthbert's in Edinburgh, where he had been an elder. Parish records reveal that, as a laird, he had in the church a loft, or gallery, and an 'isle', or burial place, underneath it. (The church building of his time has been replaced, and there is no longer a vault or grave for Napier, but a wall plaque inside the present building commemorates him.)

Napier once wrote: 'I have not done perfectly as I would, but zealously as I could.' Humble words these, and they suggest that although he was anxious to have his inventions published, he did not yearn for the fame they subsequently brought him. Yet it is sad to think that he died just before his 20 years of toil were to be rewarded with international acclaim. Napier's son Robert, the only one of the twelve children who seems to have inherited an interest in mathematics and science, undertook to publish his father's *Constructio*, which he did in 1619. This was a description in Latin of how Napier had worked out his great invention of logarithms – something he had been unwilling to reveal in his original publication. Robert wrote:

> *Since his death, I have been assured from undoubted authority that his new invention is much thought of by the most able mathematicians, and that nothing would delight them more than if the construction of his wonderful Canon, or so much at least as might suffice to illustrate it, were published for the benefit of the world.*

Briggs kept his word to Napier, and not only revised the logarithms to the base 10, which he finished in 1624, but also collaborated with Robert on the production of the *Constructio*, putting in comments on Napier's work. Robert also gathered together his father's notes and papers and put them together under the title *The Book of Arithmeticke and Algebra*, which he presented to Henry Briggs. This was most fortunate, because while a lot of Napier's papers were subsequently lost in a house fire, the book survived, and was published in 1839 by a descendant, Mark Napier, under the title *De Arte Logistica*. In this it was revealed that Napier was only at the beginning of his mathematical discoveries when he died. Among other things, he anticipated Newton in calculating the powers of numbers.

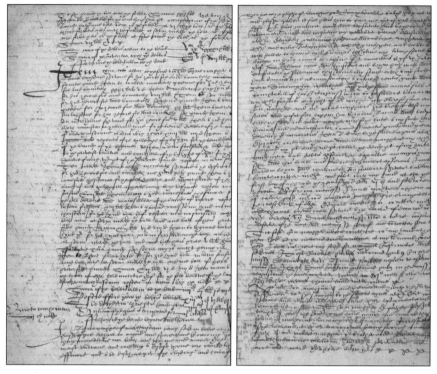

Feeling 'haill in mind and spereit', Napier dictated his will to his solicitor in April 1617 and was called 'out of this transitorie lyfe' only three days later. (Courtesy of the National Archives of Scotland. Ref. CC8/8/49)

On the continent, Kepler, unaware of Napier's death, wrote to him on 28 July 1619, giving him the highest accolade of praise. 'Now, illustrious Baron, I accost yourself apart from all others – as the subject, and your book entitled *Mirifici Logarithmorum Canon* demands ....'

By 1620 a logarithmetic scale had been invented by the Englishman Edmund Gunther, and William Oughtred began work on a rudimentary slide-rule. The first slide-rule to have a scale which moved inside a rule was produced in 1654 and used logarithms for the multiplying and dividing function.

Only a decade later, Sir Isaac Newton was sitting in a garden when an apple fell from the branch of a tree. From this simple occurrence he began working on his gravitation theories, and used Kepler's calculations to develop this work, which he demonstrated in his *Principia*. These calculations were only available to him because Kepler, in turn, had had Napier's logarithms to assist him. Today the tables of logarithms have been replaced by the scientific calculator. Clearly this is handier for mathematical working, but Napier's logarithms did not depend on batteries to function.

Napier's Bones also have their part in history, being the basis of the first calculating machine. The figures on the Bones were put on to cylinders in 1621 by Wilhelm Schickhard and the results of the sums were transferred on to a mechanical accumulator. Kepler was excited at this discovery, and put in an order for one to be made for him. Alas a fire in Schickhard's workshop destroyed this dream. It was not until the nineteenth century that progress on producing a feasible calculating machine was made by Charles Babbage. Again we have to look back to Napier for its origins.

Napier, therefore, by inventing the logarithms and the Bones, was the father of the slide-rule, a version of which was still being used in the 1970s at NASA for the development of space travel. Napier was also the father of the scientific calculator and the calculating machine. His contribution to mathematics cannot be over-estimated.

Napier's fame was at its greatest in the decades immediately after his death in 1617. Then, curiously, for nearly two centuries he seemed to slip into oblivion, except in academe. No statue of him was raised by his native city.

In 1787, however, a very scholarly and technical book, complete with mathematical graphs and tables, *An Account of the Life, Writings and Inventions of John Napier of Merchiston*, was published by the Earl of Buchan and Walter Minto. Then in 1833, Napier had a boys' boarding school named after his home when Merchiston Castle School was founded and housed in the building. (The school still thrives, although in 1930 it moved to purpose-built premises. One of the new teaching blocks, however, is called the Napier Schools.)

In 1940 St Andrews University, Napier's alma mater, opened an observatory named in his honour (right). (Photo: Ronald Hilditch)

An astronaut in space uses technology born of Napier's inventions nearly four centuries ago. (Courtesy of NASA)

In 1834 Mark Napier, with his very detailed biography, drew the attention of the world once more to his ancestor's inventions. The biggest celebration of Napier's genius, however, was on 24 July 1914, when a large gathering of mathematicians from all over the world held a conference in the University of Edinburgh to mark the tercentenary of the invention of logarithms. At this gathering papers were given, a handbook was written, sets of surviving Bones and other artefacts were displayed, and the *Napier Memorial Volume* was published by the Royal Society of Edinburgh the next year. It was no one's fault that the excitement of the conference was suddenly overshadowed when the delegates had to rush home – World War I was on the brink of being declared.

How has Napier fared in more recent times? His *alma mater*, the University of St Andrews, recognised the extraordinary achievement of their alumnus by creating a permanent lectureship in astronomy named after him, and in 1940 by opening an observatory, also bearing his name, which now houses two student telescopes. A Napier professorship followed in 1950.

Current research interests in the astrophysics group in the School of Physics and Astronomy include searching for planets around stars other than the sun; theory and observations of the formation of stars and planets and the evolution of stars in binary star systems. Napier, so interested in astronomy, would have been delighted to know that he had helped with these studies.